Reflections Of A Pondering Mind

Moiz Poonawala

BookLeaf Publishing

India | USA | UK

Made with ❤ on the BookLeaf Publishing Platform

www.bookleafpub.in

www.bookleafpub.com

Dedication

*Somewhere in the fleeting quiet moments that exist
between chaos and calm ,
the mind wanders in introspect and reflection .*

*Reflections of a Pondering Mind is a collection born from
these wanderings of the curious mind .*

*Some poems may echo your own reflections , others may
offer a different view point on your perspective .
Whichever the case , I hope they speak to you as your
companions in contemplation .*

Welcome to a journey of a mind that dared to wonder .

Preface

Every poem in this collection is a whisper from the pensive corners of my mind , thoughts that lingered too long to be forgotten, emotions too raw to be left unsaid. Reflections of a Pondering Mind is a journey through the emotional landscapes we all traverse: love and loss, hope and despair, wonder and weariness.

These words were born in solitude, in those in-between moments when the chaos and hustle of daily life somehow pause and the soul begins to speak.

Thank you for taking the time to reflect on my minds wanderings . I hope you find a few echoes of your own reflections here.

Moiz Poonawala

Acknowledgements

This book would not exist without the love, encouragement, and quiet strength of those who stood by me . Even when my words made little sense, or sometimes none at all.
To my family, thank you for your unwavering support and always encouraging me to write (especially DAD)
To my mom for passing on her poetic genes .
To my Alma Mater , St Vincent's , the institute which helped me hone my language and writing skills as a child .
And most importantly, to the quiet moments of solitude and overwhelming emotion , that gave birth to these poems . Thank you for making me look within.
This book is for all the ponderers, the dreamers, and the feelers. I see you.

Moiz Poonawala

1. The last man standing

The shrieking silence pierced my ears,
The moaning winds tried to calm my fears.
The lonely streets, stretched without an end,
Not a man, woman, child, foe or friend.

Empty spaces filled my sight,
Haunting me in that dim gray light.
Dark ashes arose, as my footsteps fell,
Dark ashes, reminiscent of the Dark Death knell.
My ears were thirsty for any mortal sound,
My eyes scoured over the Pagan ground.

But not a soul remained in the wasted land,
Not a sound besides the whispering dust and sand.
Was this the place that we called Hell,
Where Satan himself chose not to dwell !

Not many moons ago , this place was still,
A Golden paradise,
For which , mortals would fight and kill.

A place that buzzed with bees and bird,
A place alive with song and word.
Where sparkling silver streams, gurgled with joy,
And Giant Greens, sheltered creatures sweet and coy.
A place filled with joy and love,
A Home to every man and dove.

But kill, was what the mortals did,
Slaughtered one another,
Till none were left to bid.
Among themselves, the Brethren fought,
To what grim end, none gave a thought.

The kingdoms fought with tooth and nail ,
crumbling to dust , like straw castles in a gale .
Every human slaughtered , every home plundered
To what end and purpose, in horror we wondered

But , The greatest sinner amidst them all,
The one to witness the last downfall ,
All alone in this desperate desolate land ,
wishing that death had traded him a hand ,

Alas ! That burden befell me ,
For cursed I am, here still to be
The Only Last man standing free

2. Daughters

On a golden dawn , one chilly winter day
I had held you close , you stole my heart away
Your tiny crying wail and cherubic eyes ,
made a warm golden joy in my heart arise
My days were filled with love and pure cheer
At Nights you slept in my arms so tiny and dear
I had held your fingers , and you learnt to run
What beautiful days we had spent out in the sun
You looked up to me with awe and wonder ,
Cheered me up on days i was down and under !

But time it's said , flows as quick as sands
I watched you grow , as i held your tiny hands
Soon , too soon , before i knew
You were a young new leaf , fresh as morning dew !

How shall i forget that sweet sad parting sorrow
You traded my hand for a better tomorrow

You took pieces of my aching heart away
But i knew goodbye was the only rightful way
I knew that life will be the same again never
What i had cherished with love was gone forever.

Soon you took the winding road of life
Traveled far and wide to meet your own new strife
The long dusty road of life kept us far apart
But strong threads of love played their part
You were always in my heart and mind
And the same love in your eyes did i always find .

But Time they say is like flowing sand ,
Always flows faster when there's little left in hand
When i meet you now , for the shortest while ,
For a fleeting hug , to see your lovely smile
My heart fills up with a sweet sad sorrow
Will we meet again , or is this the last tomorrow
Now i know that time will be , my closest friend never,
Your every loving embrace now means more than ever

3. Milestones of Memories

Standing here , when I glance back ,
The road seems so long , have I lost all track ?
What I've left behind , in all those miles ,
A mixed blur of memories,
Love, hurt , tears and all the golden smiles .

With every passing day , a new story unfolds ,
a white quilt of memories , stitched with threads of gold
The sweet rapture of making loyal friends ,
Bitter sweet goodbyes at some unknown bends ,

Sweet memories which help our differences to mend ,
Always hoping to meet once before the end.
Moments of colossal awe and wonder ,
watching the lit skies so purple with thunder

The soft smooth touch of my first falling snow ,
Sitting beside her , watching the fireflies glitter with
glow.

Discovering a feeling that has no name ,
Wonder and awe ,
At how the tiny soul, in my arms she came

Countless tiny moments of intoxicating joy ,
Small moments of success , felt like conquering Troy.
Milestones of memories , they dot the path ,
Are not milestones all that mattered right from the start

.

All the miles in between were just a rushing blur ,
Maybe time will make their purpose clear .

One glance at the long road ahead I take ,
The path seems long and hostile to take ,

Weariness burdens my tired soul,
But I know that I must play my role .

That this book , to the end ,it must be read ,
For the sake of golden milestones , all the thorns must be
tread .

4. The book of life

When God, who wrote the fate of one
And God, who wrote the fate of all,
There was a page for this tiny soul,
Which in the Book of life did have his role.

His page began with a wailing cry,
Reminder of How hard he must try,
To keep his name in the Book of Life
A reminder of all forthcoming strife.

Though his page began at a leisurely pace,
Very soon, too soon , he would join the race.

He held his pen with steady hands,
and wrote new chapters on different lands
with ink of laughter , he wrote lines of pain,
some chapters lost, and some found again .

He started to learn, life is a strange brew,
Hurt, Anger, Pain, joy and friendship too ,
Smiles sprinkled atop, a very precious few .

All rocks and hurdles life bought his way,
He learnt to skip, above and away.

In awe he learnt to respect the strength,
Of the River of Fate, which had his every foolish pride
bent.
With wisdom he learnt to take in stride,
All hurt and pain, without burying his pride.

He learnt to live life, like the mighty kings
A king at heart, not of worldly things.
The greatest truth dawned at the end of the page,
A truth feared by even the greatest sage.

When life got as Beautiful as he could ever want,
Death fell in love, and that was the very last taunt.

5. Two flames in the wind

Darling lets spin a magic crystal ball,
Let's sit back and watch the cherry blossoms fall,
Let's snap a finger, let's just blink our eyes,
Watch the matchsticks flame say its last goodbyes !

Though its beautiful to just sit and watch,
All things beautiful, are bound by the spinning clock.
The crystal ball shall stop all too soon,
Gently the blossoms shall fall, against the bright full
moon.
The matchsticks fighting flame will soon be gone,
And its embers too in the cold winter dawn.

Time binds our lives in its gripping embrace,
Life entwines us in a maddening race.
Time spins swiftly , like a spinning top goes round,
every passing day, a dizzying dance on ground.

Just an hour back we were so young, so twenty !
With a whole new life ahead and time seemed aplenty !

But the twenties flew in a blink of our eyes,
We had barely winked, and they had said their goodbyes

With wonder i often ponder within,
Does time never stop, when did it ever begin ?

Darling i know, we are but Two flames in the breeze,
And the harsh Winds of Time, shall do as they please,

But our love is tinder for the glowing flame,
The harshest wind, our love shall tame.

Inevitable it is, and this i do know,
Two flames one day will be doused and gone,
But our cinders of love will forever linger on !

6. The wonder years

Playful Clothes , all muddy and stained ,
Fragrant monsoons from the heavens they rained !
Adventurous swashbuckling games we played
Pirates and buccaneers we often feigned !

Hands sticky from sweet stolen treats,
Hide and seek played in dusty streets !
School lunches shared under banyan trees ,
Names carved on desks, promising friends to forever be!

Oh How I wish I could return to those Wonder years !
Where we never had to hide our tears,
Our guardians shielded us from pain that sears ,
And We never warred with our hidden fears

Life was a simple open book ,
Our hearts could be read with just a glance or look !
Every tiny joy felt like a treasure trove ,
For our sorrows , nurturers were the Iron glove .

Friendships were true , our needs so few
Hearts filled with hope, fresh as morning dew !
The time we had , was our very own ,
Unlike now , every second on a loan .

But,Time like a silent thief , slowly , quietly crept ,
Age stole wonder years , while childhood like a baby
slept !

Sometimes I wonder if those years truly were ?
Or was it just a beautiful dream , a fading misty blur .

Were they a trip to some magic faraway Never never
land,
Have I now awakened from the best dreams someone
ever had ?

Now with nostalgic thoughts, my weary heart aches ,
In golden memories it finds a healing solace !

7. A thin fine line .

A thin fine line , so fragile ,so true
It lures us towards all things shiny and new ,
A thin fine line that entices and taunts
A thin fine line differs needs from wants.

Come cross me, lures the thin fine line ,
"And your happiness i will help you define ".

But the more i cross this thin fine line ,
Happiness eludes this life of mine.
"Just A little more " it jeers and taunts ,
Lets give in, to a few more wants.

Every passing day we toil and burn ,
To fulfill dreams and wants, stored in a bottomless urn
Mindlessly we hoard and plunder ,
Our wants and desires, burying us deep under

Shall we ever get free from this mindless drudgery ,
Or have our wants bound us to a life of eternal slavery ?

Wants and needs , two voices collide ,
each one jostling with our heart to abide

Wants are whispers ,so sweet and alluring ,
Promises of joy , always deceiving
Wants are deceptive,elusive and grand,
like soft white sand, slipping away through our hand.

Needs are soft whispers ,they call out every day ,
The heart's true compass, they truly guide the way.
Needs are the ones, with roots grounded and deep ,
Like an anchor on a ship , our balance steady they keep

In this tango of two , balance is key
If balance is found we shall truly be free,
when the difference in both ,we learn to define,
peace , happiness and success ,shall all gracefully align

8. Mother of mine

The first memory that i can now recall,
Is looking up at you , so pretty and tall.

I was only five , or maybe four
But holding your finger made me feel so sure.

You held my hand and walked me down tough roads
Your loving smile, a shield,from the evil wordly goads.

You meant the world, to my tiny ,weak ,soul ,
Only your love could make it strong and whole .

And that you gave so selflessly,
Every minute, every day, it flowed, almost endlessly.

I grew young and brash, as you grew old and wiser,
I wish I knew then , you were my true guide and advisor

I kept trying your patience, with my youthful blunder,
Your wise words felt like they were pulling me under.

The years passed on, and your love grew stronger,
While i wavered often, in my youthful pride and anger.

You selflessness was tested thin,
But You would never let me down, i knew from within.

Now i hold the fingers of my little one,
Like you had held mine, when we first begun !

I now know what your heart had felt
Why at my every whim you would always melt !

As I see you age gracefully , day after day,
So Grateful , you are here ,all through the way.

From the bottom of my heart i silently pray
Mother,
May your guiding beacon, forever bright and strong stay.

9. The Insignificance of US

Often I gaze at the primordial night skies ,
Boundless vast space, Timelessly still it lies.

Celestial clouds , vast and full of mystery
Nebulae and dwarf stars , with a trillion years of history

Interstellar galaxies , light years apart ,
Of this mind boggling array, Earth is but a tiny part !

On this pale blue dot , spinning in unfathomable space ,
like fleeting sparks we are born and live life's race,

and in a blink of an eye , this short life is all but spent ,
Like a candle flame its light ,to vast voids of darkness
briefly lent !

And then It sinks in , like a shocking epiphany ,
The trivial nature of all humanity !

A speck of dust in this celestial expanse ,
A grain of sand in this ethereal dance !

We Claim what ours never was ,
We build and hoard for some godforsaken cause !

Take pride in owning Lands so vast ,
Six feet we own , when our coffins are cast !

Ashes and dust are all that shall remain ,
Death looks upon , even The Greatest Leader with
disdain

No matter how vast are the empires we build ,
She treats all mortals as one common guild !

10. Magical Night

I walked along the beach one night ,
and came across this entrancing sight
An inky blue sky that night I saw,
Like a mystical beauty , without a flaw

So cloudless were the heavens that night,
A million diamonds set the sky alight .
The moon shone on the still blue sea ,
It's white light as soft as soft can be

Gentle waves , they splashed the shore ,So softly ,
silently ,
Like thousand angels whispering a magical lore

When ever I am in my darkest deepest thoughts ,
To my minds eye this enchanting sight is bought .
And like soft sand eroding on that magical bay ,
I can feel all darkness being washed away !

11. Beyond and Yonder

Does birth reflect an angels fall ?
Is death a door , or just a solid wall ?
Does the soul traverse when we dream in deep slumber ?
Often I lay awake and ponder in wonder !

What lies beyond our line of sight ,
Beyond and Yonder the cosmos so bright ?
When we fall and return to dust and ashes
Do our echoes still linger like memories in caches

Are we but dreams of a slumber deep,
Of the gods , blissfully lost in sleep!
Is all we see around and about ,
Just fleeting shadows , phantoms of doubt
Do we even exist , or just imagine all we know ?
Are we but imaginary shadows ,
cast by moonbeams glow ?

This fleeting human form, miraculously we take ,
Frugal and fragile , as reflections on a lake

What was before we were , where shall we go hereafter ?
To realms undiscovered , full of joy, cheer and laughter ?

What lies Beyond and Yonder ? Is it Heavens gate ?
An ungodly underworld ? Or a quantum twist of fate ?

We shall never know , until our time runs out
The existence of our race , what it was all about !

12. Innocence - Lost and found

Not too long back I had a friend ,
Whose smile I know I shall never forget ,

He could make this world a lively place ,
Smiles hid all pain on that innocent face

His eyes were kind , happy ,and full of life
Overflowing with joy, never scared of strife

His heart was pure , and so unstained
His spirit free , never knew restraint .

His mind so free without a care ,
His thought flew high where angels dare

His words were kind, so sweet , so pure
Like music that can heal, soothe and cure

But the winds of change , at him they tore
Re-sculpted his mind , his heart and his very core.

He seldom smiled , or spoke his mind ,
Seldom showed much care for his kind .

His friends grew few , and many were his foes
His words grew few as his pride arose.

Anger and pride consumed his very being
I Pitied the ailing soul , alone and devoid of all sheen

Now everyday I stand among my own reflections
And tell myself it's now or never ,
Change now my friend , before you are lost forever .

13. A Life taken For Granted

Ask a starving man , the true worth of bread
A pauper yearns , a piece of cloth bare-thread

A beggar salvages precious alms every single day
The mute wish , the value of speech they could voice and
portray

The blind would trade a thousand nights,
To just once see all of nature's wondrous sights.

The homeless weep and pray for a broken leaking hut ,
Wealthy men in mansions , lose peace and sleep to glut !

A blind man stumbles , in a dark perennial night ,
A crippled youth despairs, that his ailing limbs may
show some might!

A sailor's feet yearn for the touch and smell of earth,
The childless pray for a miraculous birth

An innocent prisoner craves ,
a breath of air free and fair,
Somewhere an orphan whimpers and weeps ,
yearning his parents tender loving care !

The gentle dawn wakes us with soft morning light ,
we stir awake , eyes full of dreams so bright
We wake up healthy, nimble and full of might
Yet simple blessings fade from our ungrateful sight !

A roof we have above our heads
A shelter complete with warm cozy beds
A table set , blessed with our daily bread

A friendship that weathered over the long hard years ,
Quiet moments of peace , void of stress or fears .

Laughter shared with loved ones near and dear
Simple joys that gave back colossal cheer !

A strangers smile , a quiet helping hand
fleeting moments escape our hands like flowing sand

Yet , the most trivial things we crave, mourn and miss
Often overlooking life's bounties ,so full of bliss

The truth is , those who have never had ,
Show life's not always rosy,
It can be harsh, cruel and sad !

14. A Cosmic Conspiracy

The stars softly whispered in conspiracy ,
Planets aligned in perfect coherency ,
And in the sweeping depths of the galaxies wide ,
Destiny did every law of nature abide

Through the infinite fabric of time and space ,
Among billions of souls in this vast human race ,
The cosmos knew we were always meant to be,
A bond destined since eternity

Our paths have crossed, by a swirling waltz of fate
Neither earlier than planned , nor a second too late

Life before you was like an empty book
With ink of love you filled every cranny and nook !
Like gravity draws the moon to the sea
Our souls intertwined, so naturally !

Our cosmic meeting had unfolded as planned through
time ,
So discreet and subtle , and yet so splendidly sublime !

15. Fireflies and Pixies

As Twilight falls , and moonbeams glow ,
When the fragrant winds of midnight blow ,

Night hums a gentle lullaby so deep.
Clouds turn heavy with slumber and sleep,
With the stars and moon they hide and peek,
Woods come alive , with creatures coy and meek .

Fireflies like lanterns glow , while forests fall asleep
Their golden light, casts a mellow gleam ,on the woods
so dark and deep !

They dance and flit through the deep velvet dusk ,
The Woods dance and glow , filled with fragrant musk !

Inside Giant gnarly greens , and under tangled roots ,
Arise pixie folk , and gnomes in magic boots !

Magic Pixies flit , in the twilight hush
and the Fae, they prance in the fauna lush .

Sprinkled stardust glows in their golden red hair ,
Pretty petal gowns , light as thistledown , they wear
Silver veined wings sparkle and shine , on their bodies so
tiny and fair

With Enchanting mischief they laugh and play ,
Smiling gurgling smiles , They shun all gloom away !

They chase the stars , and paint the skies ,
With purple pixie dust ,and trails of fireflies

Though no human eye may often see ,
This magical and glowing spree,
Should you choose to inhale the whispers of your soul ,
You just might hear them whisper, laugh and roll !

16. In Awe of Nature

The unconquered mountains tower with grace,
Their ancient snowy peaks adorned in a misty embrace.

The rivers carve, through stone and lime,
Never slowing down, never pausing in time

The woods are dark, deep and wide ,
Where sun and shadow dance and glide.

Silver blue streams , giggle with joy from within ,
The gnarled giants green , are home to wild woods kin

The flora blooms in colors vibrant and bold ,
A silken tapestry of red , blue and gold.

The ocean sways, a restless soul,
Its waves in endless rhythms roll.
Beyond our fathom, is the Oceans deepest depth ,
Where Secrets lay buried ,and hidden treasures are kept

The sky burns red with the rising sun
Then fades to hues of pink as the day is done
The stars they twinkle , soft and bright,
Each tells a story , filled with hope and light .
Soft moonbeams bathe the inky black voids of night
fireflies flit and grace , and glow with might

The masterpiece that's Nature , truly leaves us in awe
How Mighty are the Creators who sculpted without a
flaw ?
They gave us this treasure to guard , colossal ,awesome
and grand,
But our choices may soon leave behind , black ashes and
wasted land

17. A Fathers Wage

You held my hand , with tiny fingers frail ,
You were raw and naive afraid to fall and fail !

Your world was filled with toys and fairy tales
Together we chased paper boats with sails !

Though Your million questions had me often perplexed ,
I tried my best to never get vexed !

Your simple doubts made me smile with muse
Our often silly talks chased away my Monday blues !

You flapped your tiny arms to be piggybacked ,
Wide arms welcomed you ,never love they lacked !

You often fell asleep upon my chest ,
Your gentle embrace laid all my worries to rest !

Soon , too soon , you outgrew my arms
Watching you grow felt like soothing balms

You soon became my pillar sturdy and strong
Our roles reversed , I stood corrected where wrong

With your every success my heart filled up with pride
I Watched you grow in leaps and stride

The truth I knew I had to face one day
Dawned a bit too soon , time had its way

You parted ways , traveled to distant lands
My fingers felt you go , like soft sifting sands

The seasons whirled ,scattered us apart
Through storms and sun we played our own part

Life took us through our own joys and strife ,
Together we carved our separate paths in life

Now as you grow younger and I turn older with age ,
Son , may I ask for A fathers wage ?

When your aging father lays silent and still
You must walk on with an Iron will

Though I may not forever be by your side ,
Echoes of my existence shall always their duties abide ,

Never bow down to harsh winds that rage ,
Be sure to read life's book to the very last page

You mirror my stride , and my humble grace
Through you I hope to live through time and space .

18. Empty Nests

Where did you go , oh golden days ,
The wild , unruly, tempestuous phase !

The breakfast chaos , and the slammed back doors ,
All the backpacks strewn across bedroom floors !

The walls still trap , lovely echoes inside ,
crazy laughter and banter , when they were so close
beside.

No toys , no mess, no tangled shoes,
No tantrums no squabbles , no more treasure hunt clues
The backyard sulks in silence , where once baseballs flew
,
Bouncing glee , howling war cries ,such a lovely brew

Now silence sings ,where once chaos hummed,
Skits and plays rehearsed , and guitars wildly strummed

Now a quiet emptiness fills the same vibrant walls ,
Every Nook and corner , a priceless memory recalls .

The chapters turned , without our say,
Time is powerful, it did have its way
The hands that once braided your ponytail,
Have aged gracefully , turned a little frail.

The chapters turned without our say ,
But we still did manage to find our way .
Learnt once again ,we are two flames burning strong ,
Winds of change ,shall never leave us lonely and forlorn.

Though harsh lonely winds may batter and blow ,
All sadness shall ebb , only joy shall flow,
Our hearts with hope shall beat steady and strong ,
Birds that flew away ,shall return where they belong

19. Travel , the heartbeat of life

Weren't we born to wander and wonder within,
What lies at the very other end of earth's steady spin ?

To travel this world , to find our true worth
Find courage and valor , we never knew at our birth.

To befriend and mingle with people so new,
Explore fabled places , where only brave winds dared
flew.

Every place alive with history ,
Cobbled streets ,smell faintly of mystery !

Each turn that we take
Every bend and mistake

Holds a secret inside , a splendid tale untold
Listen softly and truly ,and watch the magic unfold

Every mountain and spring ,
bursts with life from within ,

Mighty gorges and rivers , Grasslands spreading so vast
home to kingdoms of fauna , spells of awesome wonder
they cast !

They would love to spin a splendid tale,
Of a people ancient, and memories pale

Only if we care to lend our hearts true ears
Will they share fables of ancient kingdoms, wars , and
tears !

Of civilizations and kingdoms , and eons bygone,
Of swords, shields and armors , that castle walls adorn!

Great Castles , and buildings , towering tall
How the mightiest Kingdoms , did crumble and fall

Oft have I wondered , if we were never to know,
what lies beyond the horizons alluring red glow ?

No adventures to remember, No stories to tell ,
deep regret ,wasted prospects of travel so swell

Travel is but , the heartbeat of life ,
To Settle for less , is to surrender to strife ,

So travel until your feet allow you to walk
And travel until there's still spin left in your clock !

For who knows when life's journey shall end ,
When we shall alight, at some sudden unknown bend!

20. Lost in this Connected World

Wires hum , and glass screens buzz,
Million reels they fill our heads with fuzz ,

Fake warmth and joy , sold like precious gold ,
Yet a Million hearts at night , sleep alone and cold.

We seldom care , to hear an old friends voice,
Avoid meeting them , often by our own choice

In this golden age of bits and bytes ,
Human relationships turn devoid of light .

The glass screens have charmed and hypnotized,
Our human race now stands truly zombified.

Necks heavy with burden, eyes hooked to shiny screens ,
Our minds eye hungrily , meaningless riffraff gobbles
and gleans.

Million Strangers walk on overflowing streets,
Bumping shoulders , though not one cares to greet !

No time to ask or say a kind Hello ,
How did we all end up so aloof and mellow !

To de-stress with nature, we travel thousands of miles ,
But in a race for Likes , we capture selfies and fake
smiles !

Even free moments of leisure , we choose to disown
Memories trapped in camera's, posted for reasons
unknown !

Tinder and Threads , they claim to connect,
But True love turns elusive , broken homes prove defect

The young ones lack feelings, there is no empathy ,
Love, hurt and emotions , are all mockery

Bound tight in coded networked chains,
Why cant we feel others hurt and pains ?

Why do we seldom pause to truly care?
Why cant we , our feelings, freely show and share?

The networks void spreads deep and dark inside,
Where our solitude and strife, quietly cower and hide

Though we claim to be connected as one human race ,
Aren't we just fractured souls, fallen from Gods kind
grace !

21. Tragedies of futile war

Old grouchy leaders on mighty thrones preside,
Foot soldiers helplessly salute and abide .
Old men Drunk with absolute power in hand,
Wage futile wars , to claim some godforsaken land

Leaders speak of patriotic noble cause ,
But War is often waged to hide their obvious flaws .
Steel bites bone , but not for truth,
It only robs the cradle, starves the youth

A father digs , with trembling hands ,
Dreading what lays buried in the ruins and sands ,
A doll lays torn , besides the burning flame,
His little princess , once she had a pretty name .

A Widows weeping wail, pierces hearts like an arrow,
An orphaned mother's fretful cries
Will her fighting son , see another tomorrow ?

A child pleads and clings to his lifeless dad ,
Begs him not to go , not to betray his lad .
Orphans left , to fend in this world unjust,
Father's gone, laid to rest ,in the blood soaked dust.

Tears and fears , spread like a rabid plague,
To define lines on maps , and borders vague!
What madness reigns in the cursed , war torn lands
Cities razed to rubble, and half buried hands

The soil drinks blood with unquenchable thirst,
Cheering for more, the roaring cannons burst
Filthy old men in power , fill their coffers with gold
The common man bears grief, and miseries untold!

War always leaves , souls with a scorching scar
Blissful peace eludes , in the distance far !
Like herded cattle ,we march and we fall
Never questioning why we fight at all !